The Truly Foul & Cheesy™ Mayflower Facts & Jokes

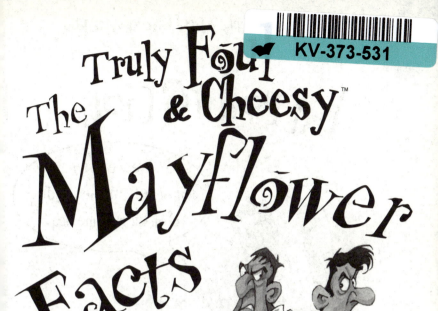

This Truly Foul & Cheesy book belongs to:

....

Written by
John Townsend

Illustrated by
David Antram

BOOK HOUSE
a SALARIYA imprint

KV-373-531

Introduction

We were so important in the making of modern America.

Warning – reading this book might not make you LOL (laugh out loud), but it could make you GOL (groan out loud), feel sick out loud or SEL (scream even louder). If you are reading this in a library by a SILENCE sign… get ready to be thrown out!

COMHAIRLE CHONTAE ÁTHA CLIATH THEAS
SOUTH DUBLIN COUNTY LIBRARIES

CLONDALKIN BRANCH LIBRARY
TO RENEW ANY ITEM TEL: 459 3315
OR ONLINE AT www.southdublinlibraries.ie

Items should be returned on or before the last date below. Fines, as displayed in the Library, will be charged on overdue items.

Published in Great Britain in MMXIX by
Book House, an imprint of
The Salariya Book Company Ltd
25 Marlborough Place, Brighton BN1 1UB
www.salariya.com

ISBN: 978-1-912537-82-2

© The Salariya Book Company Ltd MMXIX
All rights reserved. No part of this publication may be reproduced, stored in or
introduced into a retrieval system or transmitted in any form, or by any means
(electronic, mechanical, photocopying, recording or otherwise) without the
written permission of the publisher. Any person who does any unauthorised
act in relation to this publication may be liable to criminal prosecution and
civil claims for damages.

1 3 5 7 9 8 6 4 2

A CIP catalogue record for this book is available
from the British Library.

Printed and bound in China.
Printed on paper from sustainable sources.

This book is sold subject to the conditions that it shall not, by way of trade
or otherwise, be lent, resold, hired out, or otherwise circulated without the
publisher's prior consent in any form or binding or cover other than that in
which it is published and without similar condition being imposed on the
subsequent purchaser.

Created and designed by
David Salariya.

Visit

www.salariya.com

for our online catalogue and
free fun stuff.

Author:
John Townsend worked as a
secondary school teacher before
becoming a full-time writer.
He specialises in illuminating and
humorous information books for
all ages.

Artist:
David Antram studied at
Eastbourne College of Art and then
worked in advertising for 15 years
before becoming a full-time artist.
He has illustrated many children's
non-fiction books.

Disclaimer: the author really hasn't made anything up in this book (apart from some daft limericks and jokes).

He checked out the foul facts as best he could and even double-checked the fouler bits to make sure, so please don't get too upset if you find out something different from a 17th century Native American, a Pilgrim leaping off a ship or a stuffed Thanksgiving turkey.

If I had my way, I'd RATiFy the lot!

Official

warning

With the 400th Anniversary in 2020 of the sailing of the *Mayflower*, many people in the USA (especially in New England) wonder if they descended from those first Pilgrim Fathers who arrived in Cape Cod Bay in 1620. History books have long told of those brave pioneers of faith and courage who sailed to start a new great nation. However, there was more to it than that and it wasn't all plain sailing (very dodgy sailing, in fact). Before long, things turned nasty, with plenty of gruesome goings-on (and not just for turkeys).

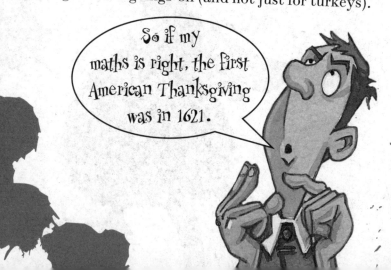

So if my maths is right, the first American Thanksgiving was in 1621.

In memory of Cape Cod, this year I've cooked cod with its eyes still in.

At least it should see us through the week.

The 400th anniversary of the first recorded American Thanksgiving feast in 2021 isn't much of a celebration if you're a turkey. They've been on the menu probably since that first feast, when other wildfowl, swan and even eagle were dished-up. Be prepared for more fowl/foul and revolting details as we now set sail on a creaky old ship into choppy waters. You have been warned…

Loopy limerick

In this gruesomely foul cheesy book
Get ready to take a quick look
At history a-plenty
From the year sixteen twenty
And a boatload of gobbledegook...

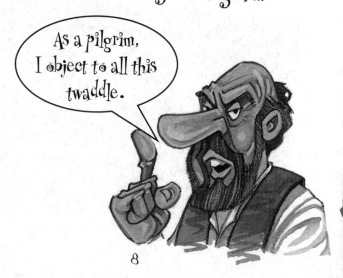

As a pilgrim, I object to all this twaddle.

What is a pilgrim?

A pilgrim is someone who makes a special journey, often a difficult one, to a distant place for religious reasons. (No, that doesn't mean a tourist to Disneyland at Christmas.)

Silly verse

We came in the ship called
the Mayflower,
We're Pilgrims* - some say
that we're quirky...
But we're tough, with
unshakeable staying-power
And a taste for American turkey.

The Mayflower
was a ship called a
carrack, with 3 masts.

We've been squabbling about religion for centuries.

*The first Pilgrims were keen to start a new life with freedom from the rules of the Church of England. Puritans were another English religious group in the 16th and 17th centuries who disapproved of the Church of England and Roman Catholics. They wanted to make worship simpler and insisted on living lives of self-control. In fact, the Pilgrim Fathers weren't strictly Puritans but 'separatists' who wanted to break away from the Church of England. Most Puritans who emigrated to North America came after 1630 in a time known as the Great Migration.

11

Fowl and Cheesy

Did you know there's an American sandwich named after some of the early settlers in America? A pilgrim or puritan is a popular snack attributed to the Pilgrim Fathers and the first Thanksgiving Day. Apparently, a traditional way of using leftover food from Thanksgiving Day was to put it between bread slices: layers of roast turkey, cranberries and cheddar cheese.

Yes, even though no cows travelled on the *Mayflower*, it wasn't long before dairy cattle were introduced to America from England. Two Devon heifers and a bull were imported to the Plymouth colony in 1623. American cheddar cheese was soon on the menu along with all that wild turkey from the woods of New England.

I've had lots of calves so I must be a Pilgrim Mother.

Q: How did the Pilgrims take their cows to America?
A: On the Mooooo-flower.

Groan

Q: Why didn't the Puritans ever talk to turkeys?
A: They were easily offended by fowl language.

Q: How much did the
   Mayflower weigh?
A: A puri-TON plus a
   pil-GRAM.

Reality Check

> So what's all the fuss about this *Mayflower* business?
> What's the big deal?
> Time for the basics…

Before the year 1600, North America was fairly quiet with very few people living there, other than pockets of native Americans (later called 'American Indians' by some Europeans). Meanwhile, Europe was packed with people in many large, ancient cities. In Britain, Queen Elizabeth I died and there were yet more arguments about how the country should be run, and especially about religion. Catholics and Protestants kept squabbling, but so did Protestants and Protestants. Some Protestants got so fed-up and worried they might get in trouble for disagreeing with everyone, that they were desperate to head off to somewhere new to start afresh. Along came a cunning plan…

In 1608, a group of English 'separatists' escaped religious persecution by moving to Holland, where their ideas would be tolerated. Dutch people welcomed the Pilgrims, as they had come to be known. Even so, the Pilgrims found it hard to settle and decided to head off to somewhere new – where they could organise things just as they wanted. Somewhere across the world without many people seemed a good idea. The plan was to set sail across the Atlantic Ocean (almost 3,000 miles) in a ship called the *Mayflower* in 1620.

As queen, I was always having rows about religion and getting rid of anyone who disagreed with me.

Fast facts

that many people don't know...

 The *Mayflower* was not the first ship of British people to emigrate to America. Others had gone several years before.

18

The only ships I can see are hardSHIPS ahead.

And strict religious worSHIP.

2 The *Mayflower* set sail from Plymouth in Devon – correct? Not exactly. It first set off from London, then to Southampton, before loading up at Plymouth and heading off to America.

South Dublin Libraries

www.southdublinlibraries.ie

The *Mayflower* wasn't due to sail alone. The Pilgrims hired a ship called the *Speedwell* to take them from the Netherlands to Southampton to meet up with the *Mayflower*. The two ships were to sail together to Northern Virginia, but the journey got off to a bad start. The *Speedwell* started leaking and had to wait for repairs at Southampton.

Both ships finally set sail from Plymouth in July, but about 483 kilometres (300 miles) from Lands End in Cornwall, they had to return to Devon to leave the still leaky *Speedwell* behind.

Some of the Pilgrims saw this as a bad sign and gave up their plans to emigrate, while the rest boarded the *Mayflower* instead, which finally sailed off on 6th September 1620. Oops – being that late meant scary autumn storms were just ahead.

It's enough to make my heart sink – and everything else.

WHAT IF

limerick

If the Mayflower had never set sail,
Would the U.S. have grown on such scale?
Without the Mayflower,
Would we now have Trump Tower?
And what of Guantanamo Jail?!

Meanwhile – on board ship as it's about to set sail, the captain was having a chat...

Susanna: Why is this ship called the *Mayflower*, Captain Jones?

Captain: No idea. If I had my way, it would be called Allied Carpets.

Susanna: Why's that, captain?

Captain: Because, like us, they always have a sail on. In fact, we have six sails.

Susanna: Do you fancy a game of cards?

Captain: Not now, if you don't mind. I'm happy just sitting on the deck.

Susanna: Why is it called the poop deck?

Captain: Have you seen all those seagulls?

Susanna: Captain, why don't you get measured for
a new hat?

Captain: Not likely, I don't want to think about
cap-sizing before we set off.

Susanna: Did you see how fast my husband rowed
the paddles in our rowing boat?

Captain: Yes, it was oar-inspiring.

Susanna: I insisted on him blowing up balloons and tying them under the hull.

Captain: Whatever floats your boat…

Susanna: There was a special offer on rowing paddles, so we bought hundreds.

Captain: That's quite an oar deal.

Susanna: I hope this ship is safe. I heard that two ships collided last week.

Captain: True. One was full of red paint and the other full of blue paint.

Susanna: I heard both their crews were marooned.

Captain: By the way, I want you to be in charge of the anchor.

Susanna: Why's that, Captain?

Captain: Because you keep sniffing and we need an anchor chief.

Susanna: Shall I weigh anchor right now?

They look like rats deserting a sinking ship.

Captain: There's no need – I know how heavy it is.

Susanna: I'm so excited to be one of your crew.

Captain: This journey will go down in history as the greatest voyage of all time.

Susanna: I used to think about time travel everyday but that's now in the past.

Captain: I was going to tell you a joke about time travel but you didn't laugh.

Susanna: I'd love to be a time-traveller. Unfortunately there's no future in it.

Captain: Doh!

For the record

Susanna White was one of the pilgrims who achieved a number of 'firsts'. She survived the dangerous journey across the Atlantic despite being over six months pregnant. She gave birth to the first surviving baby in the new colony (while the ship was still in Cape Cod Bay). She called him Peregrine. She was apparently the first person to say on arriving at Plymouth Rock, 'That's it?' Susanna also became the first bride in the new colony (just a few months after her first husband died). 1620 was quite a year for Susanna.

Peregrine means 'one who journeys to foreign lands'.

A boatload of random facts

1 The only way is Essex – for some of the Pilgrims. John Carver of Braintree hired the *Mayflower*, Christopher Jones of Harwich was captain and Samuel Fuller from Ockendon was ship's doctor. At least five of the passengers came from Billericay, including the treasurer, Christopher Martin. The town of Billerica, Massachusetts was established in 1655 to commemorate the Essex home of those first settlers.

Seasickness keeps coming over me in huge waves.

2 About 20–30 men made up Captain Jones's crew on the ship. Not all the sailors and pilgrims got on well. One of the sailors made fun of the seasick passengers and then he died suddenly. The pilgrims said it was punishment from God.

3 Each family on-board could only take a single chest of belongings. The entire journey took 66 days – just over two months.

4 At least one passenger, John Howland, was nearly killed when a storm almost swept him overboard. He was just able to grab hold of a rope and be pulled back aboard.

Yeeoow

5 Salty seawater was used for washing – but just a quick rinse rather than a proper bath. Yes, it got pongy, especially as no one could wash their clothes properly, which they wore for the whole journey (and probably slept in, too). Phewee.

6

Although there was a kitchen on the ship, most of the food would be dried or salted to stop it rotting. Most meals would be much the same, such as oatmeal, ship's biscuits, salted pork, cheese, beans and fish. To wash that down, the pilgrims drank beer – including the thirty or so children on board. Beer was safer to drink than the dodgy water. They ate hardly any fruit or vegetables. Result = chronic constipation and illness from lack of vitamins. (No 'five-a-day' – not even 'one-a-day').

The *Mayflower's* course was plotted by the captain using the stars. That took some skill as no sat-nav was available.

A baby boy, named Oceanus, was born while the *Mayflower* was on the way to North America. He later died at the age of two.

You've had the best berth on the ship.

9 A few children on board were servants. Even though many pilgrims thought their daughters were too weak to survive the hardships of the voyage, eleven girls made the trip, ranging in ages from 1 to 17 years old. Amazingly, only one young passenger (William Butten) died during the voyage. He came as a servant with the family of doctor Samuel Fuller. His master was sadly unable to help him as William was ill for much of the voyage and died just three days before land was sighted.

10 The pilgrims were hoping to land in Virginia to make their new home. The King of England had given them permission to settle around the Hudson River (in what is now the state of New York). The perilous journey and running out of supplies threw the weary sailors a bit off course so they sailed into Cape Cod Bay, without ever making it as far as Virginia.

Foul alert

(not for the squeamish)

102 pilgrims journeyed from England to the New World on the creaky ship, as well as cats, dogs, sheep, chickens, goats and a fair few rats. Imagine the smell of being cooped up with that lot for over two months, while people were being seasick. Poo buckets rolled across the decks during storms and bedding got drenched with unmentionables. The pilgrims spent most of their time crammed below decks where they ate, slept on the floor and used buckets or chamber pots. There were no windows in this area and it was often cold, damp, very dark and always smelly. Oh yes, and there was always the fear that the whole lot could sink in a storm and you'd drown. Otherwise, it was probably quite nice.

Cape Cod

Fearing the ship would be destroyed in dangerous seas, the pilgrims sheltered inside Cape Cod Bay in the early morning of 11th November 1620 and anchored in what is now Provincetown Harbour. The men spent several weeks exploring Cape Cod, trying to decide where to build their homes.

The women and children stayed on the *Mayflower*, wondering when or if the men would return. After two months, they finally found a place to settle. The harsh winter claimed many lives while the men built storehouses and living quarters. Finally, in March 1621, there were enough houses for everyone to live on land. At last the *Mayflower* left to return to England on 5th April 1621.

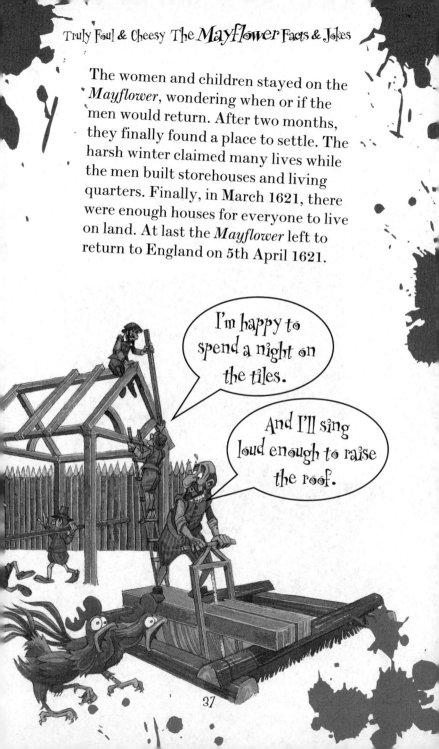

3 Cape Cod puns

Have you heard about the Cape Cod restaurant that caters just to dolphins? It only has one customer, but at least it serves a porpoise.

How do I decide on the worst joke? I'll flipper coin.

Why did the Cape Cod algae and the fungus get married? They took a lichen to each other (although, unfortunately, their marriage is now on the rocks).

Why did every Pilgrim climb off the *Mayflower* on to a rickety platform built by the crew, even though the posts in the water were giving way and they were scared? Pier pressure.

Loopy limerick

As they clambered ashore at Cape Cod
Onto soil where none had yet trod,
(so they thought)
The Pilgrims were shaken
By the sizzling of bacon...
'It's a barbecue - now that's
very odd!'
(Yes, the natives' camp fires
weren't far away.)

Foul weather & fouler times

Although the land was deserted, a few native American tribes lived nearby, so an exploring party with muskets was led by a soldier called Captain Miles Standish. Meanwhile, many of the women died from the bitter cold and diseases through the harsh winter.

My bottom is colder than an ice bucket on the shady side of an iceberg.

41

It was tough work building their new colony (called Plymouth after the port of Plymouth they had sailed from in England). Their 'Plymouth Plantation' was on the ruins of the native village of Pawtuxet.

The Pilgrims survived by stealing the food stores of neighbouring native summer villages, as well as eating corn that was still growing wild from abandoned cornfields near the ruined village. The pilgrims wrote a document called the Mayflower Compact setting down rules for living in their new community. That community had quite a few interesting characters. Meet them over the page...

It's colder than a rat catcher's heart.

Meet six of the cast...

1 Francis Billington

While the *Mayflower* was in Cape Cod Bay, teen Francis Billington was a bit of a tearaway. He and a friend got hold of his father's musket and fired it, showering sparks near an open barrel of gunpowder. It very nearly blew up the ship – which would have changed the course of history. After they'd settled ashore, members of Francis Billington's family were found guilty of all kinds of crimes, including murder. They were obviously the family you didn't want next door in a nice new colony!

I always said those Billingtons were good for nothing toe-rags.

2 Mary Brewster

Mary Brewster was the wife of the Pilgrims' religious leader, William Brewster. She was obviously a tough cookie as she was one of only five adult women to survive the first winter at Plymouth and make it to the first Thanksgiving.

3 Isaac Allerton

Isaac Allerton was something of a 'wheeler-dealer' and was among the pilgrims responsible for repaying the people back home who'd paid for their voyage. But instead, he helped himself to the funds and was banished from the colony. Somehow he survived and did well for himself – ending up with houses in both New Haven and Lower Manhattan, near where Wall Street stands today. Enough said.

4 Stephen Hopkins

The *Mayflower* voyage was Stephen Hopkins's second trip to the New World. His first was to Jamestown, Virginia, but that ship was wrecked off Bermuda (maybe the Bermuda Triangle was scary even then). There Hopkins narrowly escaped being hanged for causing trouble. He eventually returned to England, only to come back aboard the *Mayflower*. In Plymouth, he set up the first tavern, where he was fined several times for serving alcohol on a Sunday (not allowed in the Mayflower Compact). Yet again, this colourful character was getting into all kinds of trouble and being punished for breaking the rules. He certainly wasn't a Puritan.

> The rule to ban drinking was met by a chorus of booze (boos).

Oh no I'm knot!

Our fight may have ended in a TIE but you're still a loser.

5 Edward Doty and Edward Leister were servants of Stephen Hopkins. No one knows why these two Eds got into a blazing row and fought the first duel in the New World. Their punishment was to be tied together hand and foot for 24 hours. Doty spent the rest of his life in Plymouth, where he was infamous for his terrible temper. He appeared in court various times but seemed to get away with avoiding serious punishment.

Alice Mullins

6 Alice Mullins was married to shoemaker William Mullins, who brought 250 shoes and 13 pairs of boots with him on the *Mayflower*. But, although never short of shoes to wear, Alice died soon after arriving at Plymouth. Even so, she left many descendants, one of whom was the famous film star Marilyn Monroe, who also had plenty of fancy shoes, to boot (as it were).

I had to burn Alice's shoes. It was sole destroying.

At Church one Sunday

(Can you find the BIG mistake hiding in the pews?)

William Brewster: Fellow Pilgrims, we are gathered here in church this Sunday...

Mary Brewster: Sorry, love – I can't stay as I've got to cook lunch. *(dashes off)*

William: After all our trials, pilgrims, at last we have found peace and happiness...

Francis: What happens if I pull this trigger... *BANG.* Oops. *(dashes off)*

William: Can someone send for Doctor
            Fuller? It looks like Francis has
            shot one of the congregation.
            Meanwhile we'll pass round
            the money plate and take
            the collection…

Isaac Allerton: I'll happily take the collection for
                   you… *(grabs it and dashes off)*

You see, not all pilgrims were holy, honest and decent. Far from it!

Stephen Hopkins: Hey, that's against the rules of the Mayflower Compact. Anyway, what do I care – I've got to go and serve drinks in my pub…
(dashes off)

Alice Mullins: Sorry, Mr Brewster – I've got to go, too. I've come in the wrong shoes and in this snow I might catch my death… *(dashes off)*

William: Will you please all stand as we sing the hymn:

> *'Then fancies fly away,*
> *we'll fear not*
> *what men say,*
> *We'll labour night and day –*
> *to be a pilgrim.'*

Edward Doty: I'm not singing this – I'm not going to labour night and day for anyone.

Edward Leister: You've never lifted a finger. I have to do all the work.

Edward Doty: Right, that's it. I challenge you to a duel.

Edward Leister: You'll have to catch me first.
(dashes off)

Edward Doty: That's just what I'm gonna do. I can beat you by miles… *(dashes off)*

Miles Standish: Don't drag me into this – but I'll soon sort you two out… *(dashes off)*

William: Dearly beloved, we are gathered here… Oh, it looks like it's just me left. Do you know, sometimes I wonder why we bothered. *(dashes off)*

I spotted the mistake. That hymn is from John Bunyan's *The Pilgrim's Progress*, written 50 years later.

Silly riddles

Q: How did the *Mayflower* show that it loved America?
A: It hugged the shore for days.

It's so grisly here - can you bear a hug?

Q: If the Pilgrims were still alive today, what would they be famous for?

A: Their age.

Q: If April showers bring May flowers, what do May flowers bring?

A: Pilgrims.

William Bradford

We wouldn't know much about the Pilgrims arriving at Cape Cod if it weren't for one of them writing a journal. He was William Bradford, an orphan from Yorkshire. He eventually became governor in the new colony for over thirty years and wrote *Of Plymouth Plantation*, the first work of American history. This is how he told of arriving safely at Cape Cod:

'Being thus arrived in a good harbour and brought safe to land, they fell upon their knees and blessed God of heaven, who had brought them over the vast and furious ocean.

But they had now no friends to welcome them, nor inns to entertain or refresh their weather-beaten bodies, no houses or much less towns to repair to.

Ought not the children of these pilgrim fathers rightly say: our fathers were Englishmen which came over this great ocean and were ready to perish in this wilderness; but they cried unto the Lord, and he heard their voice, and looked on their adversity.' (paraphrased)

Just imagine if young tearaway Francis Billington had written a blog:

I'm gonna tell it as it is. This place is dead boring. It's a dump. There's nothing here. They call it Cape Cod but there's no fish & chips, no funfairs, no ice cream – nothing. The journey here was so gross.

That ship is one big heap of garbage – full of sick, poo, rats, wee, screaming kids, lice, fleas, maggots – and that's on a good day. They all got right stroppy with me when I let off dad's gun for a laugh. They were well-miffed and told me off for trying to blow us up. I was doing us all a favour, I reckon.

Don't pull the trigger!

Now we've landed at this slum, I hate it. There's just a dirty great lump of rock, emptiness, swamp and absolutely no night life. Believe me, nothing will ever happen here. No one's ever gonna hear of America or us again. This place is so yesterday. #*get-me-outta-here*

You just can't please some kids these days.

Just when you thought you were getting the gist of all this Mayflower history, it's time to bust a few old myths...

We're about to scrape the bottom of the barrel.

Myth 1:

The Mayflower passengers always wore black without any colour and had big buckles.

I'm not a myth - I'm a myth-ter and you're my mythuss.

Not so. Some Puritans later wore black and white, but not the original Pilgrims. When a *Mayflower* passenger died, a list of their belongings was published. John Howland had two red waistcoats. William Bradford had a green gown, a violet cloak, a suit with silver buttons and a red waistcoat. William Brewster had green drawers, a red cap and a violet coat. Children probably wore a lot of blues and yellows. And as for those tall hats with buckles that often appear in paintings... Historians tell us pilgrims didn't have buckles on their clothing, shoes or hats. Buckles did not come into fashion until the late 1600s – more likely at the time of the Salem Witchcraft trials in 1693, but that's quite another story! So, this old joke doesn't actually make sense...

Q: Why did the pilgrims pants keep falling down?
A: Because their belt buckles were on their hats.

Myth 2:

The Mayflower passengers were strict religious people who disapproved of fun, parties and enjoying life.

Not so – as some of those passengers were more concerned about starting afresh and making a better, more enjoyable life for their families by starting businesses and trade. It wasn't so much religion that drove many of them, but rather new opportunities, better chances and the hope of getting rich. Anyway, the pilgrims must have liked loud music, bands and American trad. After all, they were really into Plymouth Rock!

Myth 3:

Pilgrims lived in log cabins soon after they arrived.

Not so. The log cabin didn't appear in America until late in the seventeenth century, when it was introduced by Germans and Swedes. It seems the term 'log cabin' isn't found in print before the 1770s. Log cabins were virtually unknown in England at the time the pilgrims arrived in America. So what kind of dwellings did the pilgrims build for themselves? True, they would have used timber, but not hefty great tree trunks, just sawn planks and boards – not a log in sight.

Tougher times ahead

By mid-1621, 46 of the original 102 *Mayflower* pilgrims had died. It was local native Americans who came to the rescue. Just imagine how surprised the pilgrims were when a dark mysterious stranger turned up and spoke to them in English.

I say, how do you do, chaps?

It's terribly lovely to meet you.

A chief from an Abenaki tribe from what is today Maine was called Samoset. He had learned to speak English from fishermen who visited his camp. Fearing they were about to be attacked, the Pilgrims of Plymouth Plantation were shocked when he entered their settlement and announced, 'Welcome, Englishmen!' Samoset was friendly and offered his help.

He introduced a friend of his called Squanto from the Wampanoag tribe. Amazingly, he spoke very good English because he'd been captured by the English in 1614 as a slave and taken to Spain, but later escaped.

I've got a fowl feeling this isn't going to go well.

Fishy or what?

Squanto, also known as Tisquantum, became a trusted interpreter and guide to the pilgrim settlers at Plymouth. He taught them how to grow corn, to hunt, catch wild turkeys and to enrich the soil by burying fish heads with the seeds (nothing like a bit of fish compost to feed the crop).

It seems some of the Wampanoag people (the original natives of Massachusetts and Rhode Island) thought there was something extra fishy going on and they captured Squanto after the first Thanksgiving celebrations. Miles Standish and other pilgrims didn't want to lose their interpreter, so they promptly rescued him in a daring raid and brought him back.

Time for some drama - Much Ado About Stuffing.

I can't wait till Christmas.

Foul footnote

We don't know much more about Squanto, but it seems he became ill with a fever in 1622. His nose began to bleed and he was dead in a few days. Some historians think he may have been poisoned by his own Wampanoag people. Unfortunately, the relationship between the British immigrants and the Wampanoag went from bad to worse, with diseases brought from England, as well as attacks wiping out most of the Wampanoag. Descendants of the surviving Wampanoag people are still living in New England today.

Did you hear the one about the pilgrim and the bison?

A devout pilgrim lost his Bible soon after staggering ashore from the *Mayflower*. Three weeks later, a bison walked up to him carrying the Bible in its mouth. The pilgrim couldn't believe his eyes. He took the precious book out of the bison's mouth, raised his eyes heavenward and exclaimed, 'It's a miracle!'

'Not really,' said the bison. 'Your name is written inside the cover.'
'Where did you find it?' the pilgrim asked.
'To be honest,' the bison said, 'I burrowed it from off your shelf. You could say it was a buffa-loan!'

Mooooo

The first Thanksgiving

Thanksgiving Day is now a **BIG** event in the USA, right? And it all started from the Pilgrim Fathers in their first year in America, right? Hmmm, this is where things get messy. Be prepared to be shocked, outraged, upset, horrified or just bored to tears. Brace yourself for a few Thanksgiving **MYTHS**…

We pilgrims believe in sharing everything.

Yeah - like sharing their diseases.

Myth 1:

The first Thanksgiving was in 1621 and the pilgrims then celebrated it every year thereafter. Wrong.

The first feast wasn't repeated, so it wasn't the beginning of a tradition. In fact, the pilgrims didn't even call the day Thanksgiving. It was just a harvest supper to bring the communities together. In 1621, the Plymouth colonists and Wampanoag Indians shared an autumn harvest feast, which was probably one of the first Thanksgiving celebrations in the colonies. For more than two centuries, days of thanksgiving were celebrated by different colonies and states. What a night for fireworks on the big 400th anniversary. Thursday, 25 November 2021 will long be remembered as 'Thanksgiving 400' (until the BIG 500th!)

Do you know when Thanksgiving Day is held each year?

Myth 2:

The original Thanksgiving feast took place on the fourth Thursday of November. Wrong.

The original feast in 1621 was sometime between September 21 and November 11. Unlike the modern holiday, it probably lasted about three days. The event was based on English harvest festivals, which traditionally occurred around the 29th of September.

Myth 3:

The original Thanksgiving meal was roast turkey, cranberry sauce and all the trimmings. Wrong.

The traditional Thanksgiving menu of turkey, stuffing, mashed potatoes, candied yams, cranberry sauce and pumpkin pie wouldn't have been on the menu at that first Thanksgiving. Maybe wildfowl of some sort was there, corn, porridge and venison. It's pretty certain any sort of pie was off the menu as butter and flour were very rare, as were proper ovens for baking them. No one would have eaten with a fork, either – as they didn't have forks back then. So Thanksgiving would have been finger-lickin' good.

Gross alert

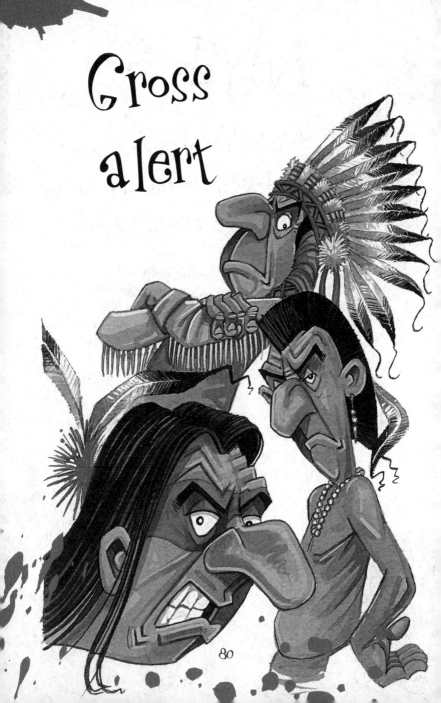

Sadly, the friendliness at that first Thanksgiving didn't last. As more European immigrants arrived (Puritans), there were many clashes with native Americans. Look away now if you're squeamish...

By 1675, Massachusetts and surrounding colonies were at war with the Wampanoag people. The Wampanoag leader, called Metacomet, was angry at the destruction of his culture and his people. He was forced to strike out and raid settlers' homes. Captain Benjamin Church tracked down and killed Metacomet. His body was drawn and quartered, and his entrails were 'left for the wolves'. His head was sent to Plymouth where it was put up on a pole for all to see. The spirit of Thanksgiving soon turned very grim.

Tragically, the new settlers also brought the smallpox virus with them. Deadly breakouts plagued local tribes and killed an estimated 90% of native people in the New England area.

Quick history lesson

The Thanksgiving holiday that most Americans celebrate today has little to do with that first sharing of a meal between Pilgrims and Native Americans. It was during the American War of Independence (from Britain) in 1777 when General George Washington asked for a day of prayer and thanksgiving. Not all states observed such a day.

No turkeys, no pumpkins, no wonder, November!

Many years later, it was President Abraham Lincoln who established a National Day of Thanksgiving in 1863. This was a plea to all Americans to have a day of prayer and thanksgiving during the American Civil War – on Thursday, 26 November. The holiday has been proclaimed by every president since, with the date changing a few times until 1941 when Congress made the 4th Thursday of November a legal holiday for a National Day of Thanks.

Why did the turkey cross the road?

To prove it wasn't a chicken.

There's always something to be thankful for on Thanksgiving. Apart from anything else, just give thanks you're not a turkey.

Please don't read this
bit if you're a turkey

Try these for some
Thanksgiving fowl figures

1 According to
people with super-
calculators and
nothing better to
do, Americans spend
something like
2½ billion dollars
at Thanksgiving
to stock up on
turkey, stuffing,
potatoes and other
holiday goodies.

2 Over 50 million turkeys will be munched to a frazzle on Thanksgiving alone (that's a lot of gobbling - about a fifth of the almost 250 million turkeys raised per year in America). Oh yes… and getting on for 50 million Americans will travel 80 kilometres (50 miles) or more for Thanksgiving dinner. Is Thanksgiving really good for the planet? (Don't even think about greenhouse gases and windy Black Friday).

Thanksgiving hymn

May your stuffing be great
And your turkey be plumped,
May the pile on your plate
Never need stomachs pumped.
May your feast be a winner
And your pies take the prize,
May your Thanksgiving dinner
Not go straight to your thighs.

I just burned
up 10,000 calories.
The roast turkey
caught fire.

Daft riddles

Q: What happened to the pilgrim who was shot at by a Native American after the second Thanksgiving?

A: He had an arrow escape.

Q: How do you keep a turkey in suspense?
A: I'll tell you later.

Q: How does Thanksgiving usually start?
A: With a T.

Q: What always comes at the end of Thanksgiving?
A: The letter G.

Q: No, really – what comes at the end of Thanksgiving?

I reckon Black Friday is a mug's game.

Real Answer: the day after Thanksgiving has been called Black Friday since at least the early 1960s. The reason for the day's name is that it's apparently the first day of the year when stores are starting to make healthy profits, so they are in the black rather than being in the red. Hence all those mad sales. It might have something to do with businesses trying to make people spend more in the run-up to Christmas, too!

You couldn't make it up

Of all those millions of turkeys killed for Thanksgiving celebrations, a couple get lucky. Every year the US President is given a turkey to be officially 'pardoned' and its life is spared. A second 'fallback' turkey also escapes the chop. A total of eight birds are randomly chosen as they hatch, which are then narrowed down to the two largest and best-behaved birds. Both birds are then spared by the president. Survival of the fattest!

Get ready to shed a tear now...
The lucky pair live happily ever
after for the rest of their days in
Virginia at George Washington's
former estate, Mount Vernon.

Turkey trots

What about the tradition of cracking a turkey bone?

The wishbone was once a symbol of luck, and the tradition of breaking a turkey wishbone for Thanksgiving started with the pilgrims, according to old legend (but more than likely it's a lot of turkey GOBBLEdegook). Yes, legend has it that if two people hold the wishbone, make a wish and break it apart, the person holding the longer piece will have their wish granted. Maybe lucky for some – but not the turkey.

Some people aren't just happy to chomp turkey drumsticks at Thanksgiving. Over recent years, people across America have taken to running around like turkeys. They take part in Turkey Trots, when they dress up as the birds and do fun runs or even marathons. Is there no end to this national obsession of upsetting turkeys?

Chickens celebrate Thanksgiving

What's the difference between chickens and turkeys?

Timeline

A final reminder about early America

1 1000 CE
Leif Ericson (a Viking
explorer) discovers
Vinland (New England).

I bet this
country won't come
to much.

2 1492

Christopher Columbus discovers the New World.

3 1507

New World named after Americus Vespucius (a Spanish explorer born in Italy).

4 1524

Verrazano (Italian) and Gomez (Portuguese) explore New England's coast.

5 1579
Francis Drake of England explores the coast of California.

I name this place Virginia - for my Queen Elizabeth of England.

6

1584
English Walter Raleigh sends the first expedition to America.

7 1604
Acadia (north east America) is settled by the French.

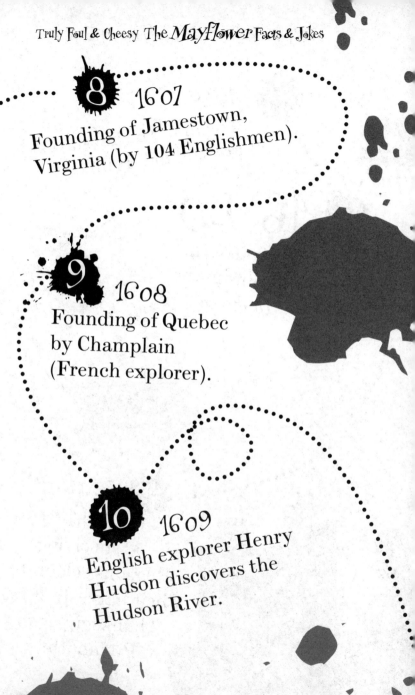

8 1607
Founding of Jamestown,
Virginia (by 104 Englishmen).

9 1608
Founding of Quebec
by Champlain
(French explorer).

10 1609
English explorer Henry
Hudson discovers the
Hudson River.

11 1619
The first African slaves are sold in Virginia.

12 **1620**
Arrival of the Pilgrims in the *Mayflower*.

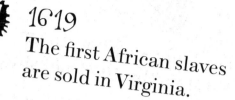

13 1621
53 surviving Pilgrims celebrate their harvest: 'First Thanksgiving in Plymouth.'

1623

Settlements start at New Amsterdam.
First settlements in New Hampshire.

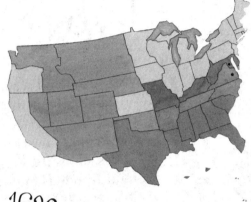

1630

The 'Great Emigration'
to Massachusetts. The
founding of Boston.

1637

War with Pequot Native
Americans. First African
slaves arrive in New England.

Just so you know...

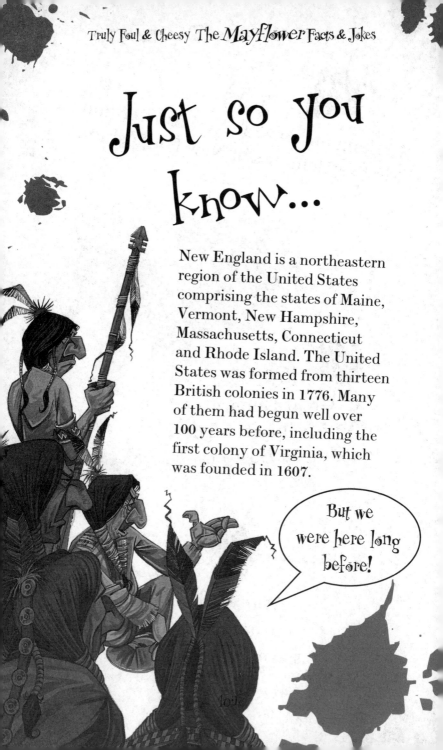

New England is a northeastern region of the United States comprising the states of Maine, Vermont, New Hampshire, Massachusetts, Connecticut and Rhode Island. The United States was formed from thirteen British colonies in 1776. Many of them had begun well over 100 years before, including the first colony of Virginia, which was founded in 1607.

But we were here long before!

And finally...

Mayflower 400 - the big party of 2020.

'Mayflower 400 celebrates the values of freedom, faith and personal liberty that informed the original journey, and which continue in the special relationship between the **UK**, **US** and Netherlands. The commemorations recognise the impact of the *Mayflower*'s journey on Native American communities and address themes of colonialism and migration, providing inclusive accounts of the *Mayflower*'s legacy.' (Thus says the Mayflower 400 organisation.)

Can you believe it?

Of the 102 *Mayflower* passengers, only 29 are known to have had descendants. But from that small number, it has been estimated that 35 million people worldwide, and 10 million in the United States, are descended today. Only about 25,000 people have been able to trace family histories back to those original voyagers. Quite a few famous people are counted among those descendants and hey, it could be YOU too!

My family tree is a walnut - most of my ancestors were nuts.

105

Last joke

The Taylor Family from Rhode Island were very proud of their heritage. Their ancestors had travelled to America with the Pilgrim Fathers on the *Mayflower*. Those pilgrims' descendants included Congressmen, successful bankers, artists, famous sports people and Hollywood stars.

On the 400th Anniversary of the sailing of the *Mayflower*, young Trixie Taylor decided to research and write a family history, something to present one day for her children and grandchildren. She found a specialist historian to help look through all the archives. There was just one problem – how to mention Great Great Uncle Jefferson Lincoln Taylor who was executed in the electric chair for his life of villainy and crime. Trixie said she could deal with their family's 'skeleton in the cupboard' tactfully. When her family history was finally published, the short section about the notorious Jefferson read:

Great Great Uncle Jefferson Lincoln Taylor was well-known by the civic authorities for his impact on the lives of many. He occupied a chair of applied electronics at an important government institution, where he was attached to his position by the strongest of ties. His death came as a great shock.

A silly play sketch

Pilgrim Father: Can you teach me how to hunt wild animals?

Native American: Sure. Would you like to hunt bear?

Pilgrim Father: Certainly not – I prefer to keep my clothes on at all times.

Native American: Ever seen a grizzly?

Pilgrim Father: Yes, my wife is always very grizzly and grumpy in the mornings. In fact, today she leapt out of bed and shot a chipmunk in her nightie.

Native American: Funny place to find a chipmunk.

Pilgrim Father: In fact, I found a skunk in my pants yesterday.

Native American: What about the foul smell?

Pilgrim Father: It didn't seem to mind. How about hunting buffalo?

Native American: It's bison round here.

Pilgrim Father: Really? What's the difference between a buffalo and a bison?

Native American: Have you ever tried to wash your hands in a buffalo? Bison can be dangerous. Always track them with care.

Pilgrim Father: You know how to follow bison tracks?

Native American: Bison leave many clues behind. Many from their behinds.

Pilgrim Father: What can you see under the feet of bison?

Native American: Squashed bison-hunters who are too slow. You pilgrims must learn respect for bison. Once they came into camp and into our tepees.

Pilgrim Father: What's that like?

I ran into a tepee and a wigwam but freaked out. The atmosphere was just two tents.

Native American: Intense.

Pilgrim Father: In tents? They actually run through your wigwams?

Native American: No, they ran. Past tense.

Pilgrim Father: Past tents? In tents? I'm confused.

Native American: Bison slept under my bed last night.

Pilgrim Father: How did you know?

Native American: I woke up with my nose on the roof of the tepee.

Pilgrim Father: And I thought waking up with mice under my bed was bad enough.

Native American: Do you know how to tell the difference between having a mouse or a bison under the bed?

Pilgrim Father: How?

Native American: If you can't pick it up by the tail, it must be a bison. There again, it could be a very overweight mouse.

Pilgrim Father: Doh!

Final teaser

If you survived some of the truly foul facts and cheesy jokes in this book, take a look at the other wacky titles in this revolting series. They're all guaranteed to make you groan and squirm like never before. Share them with your friends AT YOUR OWN RISK!

QUIZ

1. Where in America did the Mayflower arrive in 1620?

a) Cape Dolphin Cove

b) Cape Cod Bay

c) Long Island Sound

2. Why did the Pilgrim Fathers set sail on the Mayflower?

a) To start a new life together in the way they wanted.

b) To find gold and get rich.

c) To enjoy a warmer climate and better food.

3. Which English port did the Mayflower sail from?

a) Liverpool

b) Harwich

c) Plymouth

4. Who was the first baby to be born and survive in the New World?

a) Peregrine White

b) Archibald Black

c) Dorothy Grey

5. Where were the Pilgrim Fathers hoping to arrive in America?

a) Florida

b) California

c) Virginia

6. Why did over 40 pilgrims die in the first months in America?

a) From cold and malnutrition

b) From plague

c) From attacks by native Americans

7. How did pilgrims and Wampanoag people celebrate together in 1621?

a) They shared a harvest supper.

b) They held the very first baseball match.

c) They cooked a massive barbecue with a spit-roasted bison.

8. Which U.S. holiday marks that first celebration?

a) Groundhog Day

b) Memorial Day

c) Thanksgiving Day

9. Which day follows the traditional turkey feast each year?

a) Red Tuesday

b) Black Friday

c) Blue Monday

10. What happened within a few years of the Mayflower's arrival in America?

a) The first Disney World opened.

b) New York City was built.

c) Many more Europeans settled along the east coast.

Answers:

1 = b
2 = a
3 = c
4 = a
5 = c
6 = a
7 = a
8 = c
9 = b
10 = c

GLOSSARY

Colony: a territory under the control of another nation or foreign settlers.

Compact: an official agreement.

Descendant: someone who is related to a person from a previous generation, such as a grandchild of a grandparent.

Emigrate: to leave a country or region to live elsewhere.

Protestant: a branch of the Christian church which was developed in the 16th century by Christians who disliked the Catholic Church.

Puritan: a member of the 16th and 17th century Protestants in England and New England who opposed many customs of the Church of England and preached stricter moral rules.

Wampanoag: Native Americans of Massachusetts and Eastern Rhode Island, who befriended settlers until most were killed in battles begun by colonists taking their land.

INDEX

I finished reading this Truly
Foul & Cheesy book on:

........../........../..........